NFL TEAMS

CLEVELAND BROWNS

KENNY ABDO

Fly!
An Imprint of Abdo Zoom
abdobooks.com

abdobooks.com

Published by Abdo Zoom, a division of ABDO, P.O. Box 398166, Minneapolis, Minnesota 55439.

Printed in China.
052021
092021

THIS BOOK CONTAINS RECYCLED MATERIALS

Photo Credits: iStock, Shutterstock PREMIER
Production Contributors: Kenny Abdo, Jennie Forsberg, Grace Hansen
Design Contributors: Candice Keimig, Neil Klinepier

Library of Congress Control Number: 2020919478

Publisher's Cataloging-in-Publication Data

Names: Abdo, Kenny, author.
Title: Cleveland Browns / by Kenny Abdo
Description: Minneapolis, Minnesota : Abdo Zoom, 2022 | Series: NFL teams | Includes online resources and index.
Identifiers: ISBN 9781098224585 (lib. bdg.) | ISBN 9781098225520 (ebook) | ISBN 9781098225995 (Read-to-Me ebook)
Subjects: LCSH: Cleveland Browns (Football team : 1999-)--Juvenile literature. | National Football League--Juvenile literature. | Football teams--Juvenile literature. | American football--Juvenile literature. | Professional sports--Juvenile literature.
Classification: DDC 796.33264--dc23

TABLE OF CONTENTS

CLEVELAND BROWNS

Named to honor their first coach, Paul Brown, the Cleveland Browns have a strong history on the football field.

KIRKSEY
BROWNS
BROWNS

Despite several **championship** wins, the Browns have yet to reach the coveted **Super Bowl**.

KICK OFF

The Browns were founded by Arthur B. McBride in 1944. They were one of the first teams in the All-American Football Conference (AAFC).

The Browns won the AAFC **championship** four years in a row! They joined the NFL once the AAFC folded after the 1949 season.

The Browns' first NFL game was against the Philadelphia Eagles on September 16, 1950. They won, 35–10! The Browns went on to win the NFL **Championship** Game that season.

TEAM RECAPS

The Browns won its first **division** after nine years in 1980. The team played the New York Jets in the 1986 playoffs and won in double overtime! The Browns ended up losing the conference to the Broncos.

Team owner Art Modell moved the Browns to Maryland in 1995. The team changed its name to the Baltimore Ravens.

ART LIED!
ART - YOU BROKE CLEVELAND'S

Cleveland was without a football team for three years. A new Browns team was formed in 1999. In 2018, newcomer Baker Mayfield threw 27 touchdowns in his 13 starts. He broke the **rookie**-season passing-TD record held by Russell Wilson and Peyton Manning.

In 2019, the Browns finished with a 6–10 record. It was their 12th losing season in a row. Guard Joe Bitonio was named to the AP All-Pro team. His second appearance in a row.

The Browns won the 2020 **Wild Card** Playoffs against the Steelers! It was the team's first playoff win since the 1994 season. Unfortunately, they lost the **Divisional** Playoffs to the Chiefs 22–17.

BROWNS
adidas
BROWNS
adidas
BROWNS
adidas

HALL OF FAME

Jim Brown was named NFL **Rookie** of the Year in 1957. He was named the NFL's **MVP** three times. Brown set many NFL and team records throughout his career and is considered one of the greatest players. He was **inducted** into the Pro Football Hall of Fame in 1971.

Ozzie Newsome helped the Browns reach the AFC **championship** three times. He had 7,980 career receiving yards when he retired in 1990. That is a team record! Newsome was nicknamed 'Wizard of Oz' because he rarely dropped a pass.

BROWNS
73
CLEVELAND
73

Joe Thomas joined the Browns in the first round of the 2007 draft. He made NFL history when he became the first offensive lineman named to the Pro Bowl in each of his first eight years on the field!

GLOSSARY

championship – a game held to find a first-place winner.

division – a group of teams who compete against each other for a championship.

induct – to admit someone as a member of an organization.

MVP – short for "most valuable player," an award given in sports to a player who has performed the best in a game or series.

rookie – a first-year player in a professional sport.

Super Bowl – the NFL championship game, played once a year.

Wild Card Round – the first round of the playoffs. Each of the two conferences send four division champions and three wild-card teams to its postseason.

ONLINE RESOURCES

Booklinks
NONFICTION NETWORK
FREE! ONLINE NONFICTION RESOURCES

To learn more about the Cleveland Browns, please visit abdobooklinks.com or scan this QR code. These links are routinely monitored and updated to provide the most current information available.

INDEX